FORTY YEARS OF SERVICE

DANIEL COLLAMORE HEATH

FORTY YEARS OF SERVICE

Published in Commemoration
of the Fortieth Anniversary of
D. C. Heath and Company

Forty years of fruitfulness
Forty years of following every forward
movement in education by furnishing
the necessary manuals to hold it steady
Forty years of encouraging school men
to summarize experience and to give it
to the profession
Forty years of faith in the common
schools and their teachers

WM. MCANDREW

5694

D. C. HEATH AND COMPANY

BOSTON   NEW YORK   CHICAGO   LONDON
ALTANTA   DALLAS   SAN FRANCISCO

TO THE MEMORY OF

DANIEL COLLAMORE HEATH

practical idealist and maker of good books; to the
authors whose genius and labor have made the Heath
imprint a guarantee of excellence; to the employees
who during four decades have served loyally and
faithfully that the Company might fulfill its mission;
and to the millions of students and teachers who
have found guidance and inspiration in Heath books

THIS VOLUME IS DEDICATED

5694

FORTY YEARS OF SERVICE

FORTY YEARS OF SERVICE

THE publisher who supplies the tools with which the teachers of a country work renders a service unexcelled in its value to the public weal, in its influence towards shaping the character and ideals of the people. The old saying, "Let me write the songs of a nation and I care not who makes its laws," suggests a great truth. With equal fidelity to truth it may be altered: "Let me publish the text books of a nation and I care not who writes its songs or makes its laws." More than all the newspapers, more than all other books, more than the moving pictures and the radio, the text book is a constant and formative influence on the growing mind of youth from the kindergarten to the university. In the text books, from the primer to the scholarly treatise, is found the reading matter of our people in their most impressionable years, when their minds and characters are being formed. The ideals which control the publisher who furnishes this reading matter are the ideals indelibly impressed on the public mind.

The House of D. C. Heath and Company looks back upon its forty years of service to the public with a feeling of confidence that from the time when Daniel Collamore Heath planned to issue his first book, down to the present moment, it has been controlled by a steady sense of its opportunity for service and of its responsibility.

The founder of the House of D. C. Heath and Company was a man of high ideals of public service; he was a man also of broad ideas, far in advance of his time in his conception of what education should be. He believed that a broader, more humane, more inspiring type of education than then prevailed was necessary for the social and political stability of the country. He believed that it was the duty of the publisher to place in the hands of the teacher books that were not only of sound quality but books that looked towards the future, books that livened the dead routine of the schools, books that would bring to the schools the larger purposes of education and of life.

The House of D. C. Heath and Company has consistently endeavored to maintain those ideals of service to the public through the publishing of books that would exert a wholesome influence on the youth of the country. It has endeavored to contribute to the progress of education through placing in the hands of teachers the books that would keep them abreast of all advances in educational method. And it has endeavored so to conduct its own business as to inspire and merit the confidence of the great educational public in its high ideals and purposes. It is content to have its success measured by the degree of confidence which that public continues to bestow upon it.

In this forty years of service two men of broad vision and high purpose have set the standards and led the way: Daniel Collamore Heath, the founder, and his successor, William Edmond Pulsifer.

DANIEL COLLAMORE HEATH

1843–1908

DANIEL COLLAMORE HEATH

M R. HEATH, the founder of the House of D. C. Heath and Company, was born in Salem, Maine, October 26, 1843. When he was thirteen years of age his father removed to Farmington, Maine. Here Mr. Heath attended Farmington Academy, where he acquired an ambition to secure a higher education. His father was a blacksmith in humble circumstances, and education represented for young Daniel years of grilling work and self-denial. At the age of sixteen he taught school in the Currier District in Farmington, and subsequently for several terms in Farmington, Strong, and Moscow. His summers were filled with hard work in his father's shop, in the local freight office, or on some neighboring farm. His preparation for college was received in the Nichols Latin School at Lewiston, Maine, and the Maine State Seminary, which later became Bates College. He entered Amherst College and graduated with the class of 1868.

For two years following graduation Mr. Heath was the Principal of the High School in Southboro, Massachu-setts. Later he attended the Bangor Theological Seminary for two years, but was compelled to abandon his plans for the ministry because of ill health. He then spent a year in European travel, most of which time was devoted to Switzerland. He had hoped that a year of rest and travel would restore his health, but he returned home little improved.

Soon thereafter he served for a year as Superintendent of Schools at Farmington, Maine. While in this position he carefully studied the needs and conditions of the schools and wrote an annual report which is remarkable for the fact that in it he anticipated many of the modern developments in organization, methods, and curricula, especially in connection with the problems of rural schools. This report was printed and attracted wide attention.

In 1874, after spending some time on his father's farm at Farmington, Mr. Heath decided to go to California to recover his health. When he reached Boston he stopped to pay his respects to Mr. Edwin Ginn of the publishing house of Ginn Brothers, who had been greatly impressed with the report written by Mr. Heath during his Superintendency at Farmington. Mr. Ginn proposed to Mr. Heath that he visit the larger towns on his way west in order to represent the publications of Ginn Brothers. This Mr. Heath decided to do, and by the time he had reached Rochester, New York, he had met with such success that he was induced by Mr. Ginn to give up his trip to California and remain in the book business. Mr. Heath opened a New York Office for Ginn Brothers and later became a partner in the firm known as Ginn and Heath.

In 1885 this partnership was dissolved, and Mr. Heath within the same year established the publishing house of D. C. Heath and Company, of which he remained the

Head until his death in 1908. Before beginning active operations as a publisher he went to Europe in search of authors who might contribute to his list of publications, and a year later with those he had taken over from the firm of Ginn and Heath his list had reached the number of twenty-four volumes, including books and pamphlets.

Mr. Heath was a man of the deepest religious convictions and never lost his interest in religious progress. He was a member of many social and learned societies and took an active interest in public and social service in Boston and Newton, Massachusetts. He was a frequent visitor to Europe, and few American publishers were more warmly welcomed than he in England, Germany, and France. He was an ardent lover of books, an earnest student, a genuine educational reformer, and a man of rare sympathy and personal charm.

W. E. Pulsifer

WILLIAM EDMOND PULSIFER

WILLIAM EDMOND PULSIFER

WILLIAM EDMOND PULSIFER

MR. PULSIFER, who became President of D. C. Heath and Company in 1910, was born in Sumner, Maine, April 16, 1852, of good old New England stock. He was fitted for college at Kent's Hill Seminary in his native state and at Westbrook Seminary, Deering, Maine, from which he graduated in 1870. At the age of seventeen Mr. Pulsifer began that direct contact with education which he has continued without abatement to the present day. He taught in several country school districts in Maine, and during the summer months worked wherever he could find an opportunity in order to earn money enough to pay for his further education. He studied at Bates College, Lewiston, Maine, and in 1898 received from that institution the honorary degree of Master of Arts.

In 1874–1875 Mr. Pulsifer was Principal of West Lebanon, Maine, Academy; for eight years after that was Principal of the Stoughton, Massachusetts, High School, and from 1883 to 1885 was Superintendent of Schools at Leominster, Massachusetts. Then he became a New England representative for the publishing house of Ginn and Heath, which later became Ginn and Company, and remained with that firm until 1889.

In 1889 Mr. Pulsifer joined D. C. Heath and Company. First as a partner, from 1889 to 1895, then as Treasurer of the Corporation, from 1895 to 1910, and as President from 1910 to the present time, he has largely and increasingly aided in directing the policies of D. C. Heath and Company almost from the days of its inception. For the past fifteen years his mind and heart have been the motive power and the guiding force in the Company's continuous growth and development. The preëminence of D. C. Heath and Company in the educational field is due in large part to his masterful guidance.

Mr. Pulsifer's many contributions to American education, given both personally and through the publishing house of which he is the President, have been recognized frequently by educational and other learned societies. Thus, in 1920 he was elected to membership in the Phi Beta Kappa Society by the Mother Chapter at the College of William and Mary, and only recently the Board of Overseers of Harvard University chose him as a member of the Visiting Committee of the Department of Romance Languages and Literatures.

For several years he has been a Director of the National Association of Book Publishers and a member of its Bureau of Copyrights. He has been a close and discerning student of American life and of history and literature, and is the author of several historical pamphlets on significant characters, notably Lincoln, Grant, Webster, Hamilton, Jefferson, Aaron Burr, and Edmund Spencer. It is doubtful if there is any publisher who has done more than Mr. Pulsifer to give to the publishing of educational books the high standing and the dignity that this branch of publications now commands in America.

Those who know him best are one in recognizing that he possesses that rare combination of qualities which makes for permanent and deserved success. He has the ripe judgment and the wise prudence that come only with years, combined with the aggressiveness and inventiveness of youth. In his personal relations Mr. Pulsifer is a man of rare charm, whom men respect and love to follow. His most important decisions are tempered by human kindness and lightened by the saving grace of humor. He is a tireless worker who never spares himself, a hater of sham and hypocrisy, and the most loyal of friends.

E. C. HILLS

HISTORICAL DETAILS

WILLIAM E. PULSIFER   DANIEL C. HEATH

WINFIELD S. SMYTH   CHARLES H. AMES

MR. HEATH AND HIS FIRST PARTNERS

HISTORICAL DETAILS

THE House of D. C. Heath and Company was established in 1885 by Daniel Collamore Heath, who for several years prior to that time had been associated with another publishing firm, Ginn Brothers, which afterwards became Ginn and Heath. For the first few years he was without partners or associates in any positions of responsibility.

In 1888 Mr. Heath admitted to partnership with him Mr. Charles H. Ames, who has been described by Dr. A. E. Winship as "the most lovable, manly character I have ever known." Like Mr. Heath, he was an Amherst man. He had worked his way through college, and after graduation had spent fifteen years with another publishing house. He died in 1911. In 1889 Mr. William E. Pulsifer became the second associate of Mr. Heath and soon thereafter was made the Manager of the New York office of the Company. In 1893 Dr. Winfield S. Smyth was also admitted to the partnership. Dr. Smyth was a man of outstanding ability and scholarship, who had been Principal of Casanovia Academy. Upon entering the firm he took charge of its Chicago office, which he conducted with signal success for fifteen years. He died in 1908.

In contrast to the small beginnings of the House in capital and books there stood out in the strongest relief

WINFIELD S. SMYTH   FRANK F. HUMMEL

JAMES C. SIMPSON   WILLIAM E. PULSIFER

the character and ability of the four original partners who shaped the policies of D. C. Heath and Company.

In November, 1895, the partnership was changed to a corporation, the officers of which were:

> Daniel C. Heath, President
> Winfield S. Smyth, Vice President
> William E. Pulsifer, Treasurer
> Charles H. Ames, Secretary

The death of both Mr. Heath and Dr. Smyth in 1908 brought about important changes in the business control of the Company. In 1910 Mr. Pulsifer and two associates, Mr. Winfield S. Smyth and Mr. William H. Ives, purchased from the Heath estate its entire holdings of the Company's common stock. From 1910 to 1922 the following Officers served continuously on the Board of Directors:

> William E. Pulsifer, President
> James C. Simpson, Vice President
> Winfield S. Smyth, Treasurer
> Frank F. Hummel, Secretary

Mr. Simpson served as Secretary from 1911 to 1913, when he was succeeded as Secretary by Mr. Hummel. No other change was made in the Officers or Directors until the beginning of 1923, when, after the death of Mr. Simpson (1922), Mr. Smyth became Vice President, and the Board was increased to five members by the addition of Mr. Dudley R. Cowles and Dr. Elijah C. Hills. From

E. C. HILLS WINFIELD S. SMYTH

FRANK F. HUMMEL WILLIAM E. PULSIFER DUDLEY R. COWLES

1923 to the present time the Officers and Directors have been:

William E. Pulsifer, President
Winfield S. Smyth, Vice President and Treasurer
Frank F. Hummel, Secretary
Dudley R. Cowles
Elijah C. Hills

A significant addition to the organization was made in 1920 by the creating of a Board of Associate Directors for the purpose of keeping the Directors in closer touch with the now large and widely distributed number of members of the staff throughout the country, and of giving those members a more intimate insight into the purpose and policies of the Directors. The following persons were elected to membership in 1920 and 1921 and composed the original Board:

A. J. Burdett   A. G. Odell
G. H. Chilcote   L. McTurnan
D. R. Cowles   A. D. Perkins
C. H. Douglas   P. A. Ray
E. W. Harvey   A. M. Strong

The present membership of the Board of Associate Directors is as follows:

A. J. Burdett   A. G. Odell
G. H. Chilcote   F. W. Scott
C. D. Daniel   Orville Simmons
E. W. Harvey   A. M. Strong
Carl McGannon   A. B. Wright

G. H. CHILCOTE

C. D. DANIEL

A. J. BURDETT

E. W. HARVEY

CARL McGANNON

A. G. ODELL

ORVILLE SIMMONS

F. W. SCOTT

A. M. STRONG

A. B. WRIGHT

BOSTON OFFICE

50 Beacon Street

The Editorial Staff of D. C. Heath and Company includes the following members:

Dr. Frank W. Scott, Editor in Chief
Orville Simmons, Associate Editor
Dr. E. C. Hills, General Editor for Modern Languages
Dr. Alexander Green, Associate Editor for Modern Languages
Nellie E. Aldrich, Assistant Editor for Modern Languages
Dr. José Padín, Editor for Latin-American Publications

The first office of the Company was opened by Mr. Heath in Tremont Place, Boston, in 1885. About a year later he moved the business to 5 Somerset Street, and several years thereafter to 120 Boylston Street. Since 1914 the Boston office of this pioneer institution has occupied a building at 50 Beacon Street, on the site of the home of the first white settler of Boston, William Blaxton.

In 1887, two years after its establishment, the growth and prospects of the business brought about the opening of offices in Chicago and New York. The Chicago office occupies its own commodious building at 1815 Prairie Avenue.

The New York office, which, since Mr. Pulsifer became President, has been the editorial headquarters of the Company, occupied quarters in several localities until January, 1908, when, after being burned out, it was moved to 231–245 West 39th Street, where it remains.

The constant growth of the business necessitated the opening of offices of the Company in San Francisco (in 1921) and in Atlanta (in 1922).

CHICAGO OFFICE

1815 Prairie Avenue

The foreign business of the Company has had a steady and wholesome growth. Almost immediately after the establishment of the House of Heath a London representative was secured to handle in England and other British possessions of the Eastern Continent the business of D. C. Heath and Company. Later George G. Harrap and Company of London took over the agency for the British territory, with the exception of Canada.

Beginning with the Spanish-American War, D. C. Heath and Company developed its list of books for the Philippines, Porto Rico, and Latin-America. The House has also enjoyed steadily increasing sales in China and Japan. Its business in all these countries has grown until it now constitutes an important part of the Company's total business and has made the name of Heath familiar to millions in Latin-America and the Orient.

NEW YORK OFFICE

231-245 West 39th Street

A PIONEER PUBLISHING HOUSE

A PIONEER PUBLISHING HOUSE

THE House of D. C. Heath and Company entered the field of educational publishing at an eminently psychological time. Learning by rule and rote had become the fashion of the day. History meant the memorization of names, dates, and military deeds. The teaching of languages was, in the main, restricted to the acquisition of grammatical rules and definitions. The presentation of scientific facts had reached a low ebb of interest that bade fair to eventuate in dormancy. The very foundation of sound educational practice hung in the balance by reason of uncertainty as to the best course that should be pursued. The time was ripe for a new orientation— a change in the content as well as the methods of teaching— and when it came, as it was bound to come, it found in the new House of D. C. Heath and Company a ready and sympathetic ally.

Twenty-four books and pamphlets—the entire list of this Company in 1886—made but a modest beginning. An examination of their titles, however, reveals the fact that a *pioneer* force had entered educational publishing and that this new House of Heath was prepared to furnish the teaching profession the tools of the new education.

No less than one-half of the original twenty-four titles belonged to the field of SCIENCE. This is a significant index of the foresight of the House of Heath and of its firm belief that science was destined to occupy a larger

ATLANTA OFFICE

63 North Pryor Street

and more important place in American education. During
the span of forty years since the publication of these pioneer
books in science this Company has issued such epoch-
making publications as Remsen's *Chemistries*, which en-
listed the coöperation of an internationally prominent
scholar, Newell's *Chemistries*, in which the facts of the
science are skilfully interwoven with practical experi-
ments, Lincoln's *Physical Chemistry*, Venable's *Brief Ac-
count of Radio-Activity* and *History of Chemistry*, and
Hopkins' authoritative *Chemistry of the Rarer Elements*.
Colton's *Physiologies* and *Zoölogies*, which marked a new
era in the teaching of physiology and zoölogy in the high
schools and colleges, Tower and Lunt's *Science of Common
Things*, Grabau's *Geology*, and Allen and Gilbert's *Textbook
of Botany*, all of which books, among others, D. C. Heath
and Company has published in support of the new movement for *combined* scientific knowledge. The publication
of this representative list of science books bears eloquent
tribute to the House's foresight in providing for teachers
and students a series of science text books written by
advanced thinkers and scholars who blazed the way for
what is now the generally approved method of teaching
science.

LONDON OFFICE

39–41 Parker Street, Kingsway

Some of the authors of science text books who have honored D. C. Heath and Company with their work are as follows:

IRA REMSEN

Ira Remsen
Charles Baskerville
W. R. Orndorff
A. T. Lincoln
Lyman C. Newell
B. S. Hopkins
Francis P. Venable
A. W. Grabau
N. S. Shaler
B. P. Colton
T. W. Galloway
Charles E. Allen
Edward M. Gilbert
C. E. Turner

LYMAN C. NEWELL

Two only among the original twenty-four titles were in the field of HISTORY, ECONOMICS, and POLITICAL SCIENCE, but they marked a decided departure in scope of content and manner of presentation. The emphasis was shifted from desultory dates and facts to a comprehensive consideration of national and world movements, to the teaching of prime motive forces in politics, industry, commerce, and culture, and to the combination of historical accuracy and correct perspective with lucidity of style. These principles, which have been embodied in the *Bourne and Benton*, *Thompson*, and *Webster History Series*, have powerfully contributed towards assuring history the place of eminence and general interest which it holds to-day in the curricula of our schools

HENRY E. BOURNE

THOMAS J. LAWRENCE

ELBERT J. BENTON

WADDY THOMPSON

HUTTON WEBSTER

SOME AUTHORS IN HISTORY AND LAW

Outstanding pioneer books in the field of public affairs issued by D. C. Heath and Company include Woodrow Wilson's *The State*, Charles Gide's *Principles of Political Economy* and his *Political Economy*, Gide and Rist's *History of Economic Doctrines*, Alvin S. Johnson's *Introduction to Political Economy*, Frank Tracy Carlton's *History and Problems of Organized Labor*, Thomas Nixon Carver and Henry Bass Hall's *Human Relations*, Arthur W. Dunn's *The Community Civics Series*, and Thames R. Williamson's *Problems in American Democracy*.

Prominent among the Heath authors in history, economics, and political science are the following:

WOODROW WILSON

Woodrow Wilson
Thomas J. Lawrence
Edward Elliott
Charles Gide
Alvin S. Johnson
Frank T. Carlton
Frederick M. Fling
Dana C. Munro
Charles R. Henderson
T. R. Williamson
Arthur W. Dunn
Henry E. Bourne
Elbert J. Benton
Waddy Thompson
Hutton Webster

CHARLES GIDE

In the field of MATHEMATICS the House of D. C. Heath and Company laid the foundations of a nation-wide prominence which it has constantly enjoyed. Bowser's pioneer treatise on *Trigonometry* is still referred to as epoch-making

in its pedagogical principles. The House of Heath was the first to publish a series of arithmetics that pointed the way to the present-day method of teaching, by abandoning the old topical plan. The Walsh *Spiral and Semi-Spiral Methods in Arithmetic*

WEBSTER WELLS

WALTER W. HART

dominated the teaching of the subject for an entire generation, to such an extent in fact that no modern text book in arithmetic can claim to be wholly free from the salutary

JOHN H. WALSH

influence of the Watson and White continued and extion of path-find *Wells* and the *Series of Secondary* text books, distinmedium between method and teachtation, have earned

Walsh Series. The *Arithmetics* have tended this trading, while the *Wells and Hart School Mathematics* guished by a happy rigorousness of ability of presena reputation that extends from coast to coast.   The Wells and Hart *Algebras* are now more extensively used than any others in the United States.

The most representative authors of Heath mathematical text books are as follows:

G. A. OSBORNE

Webster Wells
Walter W. Hart
W. Benjamin Fite
E. W. Nichols
W. A. Wilson
J. I. Tracey
George N. Bauer
W. E. Brooke
L. C. Karpinski
George A. Osborne
Abraham Cohen
Heinrich Burkhardt
George E. Atwood
W. S. Sutton
John H. Walsh
Henry Suzzallo
Bruce M. Watson
John A. Miller
E. M. Winger
Gardner C. Anthony

W. S. SUTTON

But perhaps in no other field was this pioneer spirit of the House of Heath more manifest than in that of modern languages.   At a time when America's participation in international welfare and commercial relations was as yet visioned only by thinkers and dreamers, Mr. Heath clearly foresaw the need of broader foundations and larger expan-sion, in order to satisfy the educational demands of the

W. H. FRASER

J. SQUAIR

F. DE ONÍS

E. C. HILLS

J. D. M. FORD

SOME MODERN LANGUAGE AUTHORS

future. As a preliminary step, a list of questions was sent by Mr. Heath to every important teacher of French and German in the United States. It was probably the first educational questionnaire ever sent out in this country by a private individ-ual. So carefully were the queries framed and so detailed was the information requested that the replies covered the re-quirements and opportunities of the entire field of modern language teaching and served as a guide for the development of HEATH's MODERN LANGUAGE SERIES,

C. H. GRANDGENT

E. S. JOYNES

which, under the sym-pathetic direction of Mr. Pulsifer, the successor to Mr. Heath, has gained a reputation for completeness and serviceableness second to none in the United States. Side by side with the long famous Joynes-Meissner *German Grammars* there ranged themselves the internationally known Fraser and Squair *French Grammars* and the Hills and Ford *Spanish Grammars*. The success of all these is accounted for by the fact that they were the first to adapt the teaching of modern languages to the specialized needs of American high schools and colleges. This House, which to-day has comprehensive lists of text books in French, German, Italian, and Spanish—and publications even in Danish, Portuguese, Russian, and Esperanto—has kept steady pace with progressive ideas and has drawn to itself the most distinguished authors that have been associated with the development of modern language study.

Outstanding among the authors of *Heath's Modern Language Series* are the following:

W. H. Fraser	Ernest Lavisse
J. Squair	F. de Onís
E. C. Hills	L. A. Wilkins
J. D. M. Ford	E. H. Wilkins
C. H. Grandgent	Rudolph Schevill
Calvin Thomas	James Geddes
Edward S. Joynes	C. H. C. Wright
Irving Babbitt	G. T. Northup
J. E. Mansion	G. N. Henning
B. L. Bowen	Albert Schinz
C. Fontaine	A. R. Hohlfeld
D. H. Carnahan	C. H. Handschin
I. H. B. Spiers	J. T. Hatfield
F. M. Warren	Alcée Fortier
V. E. François	W. G. Howard
J. E. Matzke	Kenneth McKenzie
T. A. Jenkins	M. Romera-Navarro
E. C. Wesselhoeft	Ernesto Nelson
A. W. Spanhoofd	Marguerite Clément

"Know thou thyself." Two of the books in the original Heath list were designed as helps to teachers. These two volumes were the pioneers of *Heath's Pedagogical Library*, whose challenging query, "Thou that teachest another, teachest thou not thyself?" has done much to awaken a professional spirit among American teachers. For the first time within their experience a series began to appear which gave teachers not only authoritative trans- lations of standard pedagogical works from the pens of Comenius, Com- payré, Herbart, Pestalozzi, and Rousseau, but also a large number of helpful treatises in the field of more modern, practical pedagogy and edu- cational efficiency. Dewey's *How We* *Think*, Paulu's *Diagnostic Testing,* and Turner's *Es-* *sentials of Good* *Teaching* are but a few among the many vital publications that have grown out of the far-seeing aim of the House of Heath.

G. STANLEY HALL

Among the most notable authors of Heath's pedagogical books are:

JOHN DEWEY

John Dewey
G. Stanley Hall
John Adams
G. Compayré
Charles De Garmo
Will S. Monroe
Edwin A. Turner
Clarence T. Gray
Frederick Tracy
Lotus D. Coffman
Emanuel M. Paulu
Paul E. Belting
F. M. Morehouse
Horace A. Hollister
Ralph W. Pringle
John E. Stout

LOTUS D. COFFMAN

HIRAM CORSON

MARY F. HYDE

J. M. D. MEIKLEJOHN

R. G. MOULTON

W. M. PAYNE

A FEW AUTHORS IN THE ENGLISH SECTION

Yeoman service has also been performed by D. C. Heath and Company in the dissemination of texts in the ENGLISH LANGUAGE AND LITERATURE. The earliest series of English books issued by this Company for use in elementary schools was Hyde's *Practical Lessons in English.* In its long career this series has been one to conjure with. It has, beyond a doubt, had more state adoptions than any other English series ever published. Its sales to date have reached the staggering total of eleven million copies. The great popularity enjoyed in more recent years by the *Manly-Bailey-Rickert Language Series* and the Heath, Haliburton, Gordon, and Kendall *Readers* for elementary schools and by the *Buhlig English Series* and Woolley's *Handbook* for secondary schools and colleges, to mention but a few of the hundreds of Heath's English publications, is an earnest of the fact that the preëminence of D. C. Heath and Company in English has been successfully maintained.

S. V. SANFORD

E. C. WOOLLEY

Notable in this department is the *Belles Lettres Series*, now including about fifty titles, ranging chronologically from Beowulf to Tennyson, and in subject matter from the Gospels in West Saxon to outstanding examples of

Restoration Drama. This series was one of the earliest planned by Mr. Heath, to promote scholarship in the field of English, and its list of editors includes many of the most distinguished American and English scholars in the field.

The *Arden Series* of the Plays of Shakespeare is another notable item on the English list, including in the editors of the twenty-four plays already published many of the leading Shakespearean scholars and placing in the hands of students the plays of the greatest dramatist edited from a distinctly literary point of view.

Some of the outstanding authors of Heath's English publications are as follows:

C. H. Herford	Richard Burton
Edwin C. Woolley	Richard G. Moulton
John M. Manly	J. M. D. Meiklejohn
Stuart P. Sherman	Charles Eliot Norton
Felix E. Schelling	Katherine Lee Bates
Albert S. Cook	Edward Everett Hale
George P. Baker	James W. Bright
Raymond M. Alden	Vida D. Scudder
Ashley H. Thorndike	William Henry Hudson
George E. Woodberry	Austin Dobson
Rose A. Buhlig	John W. Cunliffe
Mary F. Hyde	Hiram Corson
S. V. Sanford	T. M. Parrott
William Morton Payne	Frederick S. Boas
H. F. Harrington	Frederick Klaeber

Probably no other name in the field of classical scholarship in America has meant so much as that of Basil L. Gildersleeve, and the Gildersleeve and Lodge texts have long occupied a high place in the esteem of teachers of Latin, as have other books among the Heath Latin texts. Prominent among the authors of Heath's LATIN text books are:

Basil L. Gildersleeve
Gonzales Lodge
Bernadotte Perrin
Jesse B. Carter
Harry L. Wilson

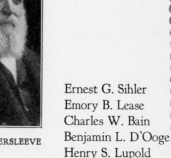

Ernest G. Sihler
Emory B. Lease
Charles W. Bain
Benjamin L. D'Ooge
Henry S. Lupold

B. L. GILDERSLEEVE

This tale of pioneering could include many other fields of endeavor wherein D. C. Heath and Company has blazed the trail for sound instruction. The story, from whatever angle it be told, is one of broad outlook, courage in pioneering, and steadfastness in sustaining the best tendencies of educational progress.

"Better Bookmaking" has from the first been one of the Company's outstanding ideals. A good book loses half its excellence if it is not visually worthy of its contents. No care or expense is spared to illustrate Heath publications with line drawings, halftones, color plates, diagrams, and maps whenever such features can contribute to the serviceability or interest of the contents. Unremitting study is made of the investigation of psychologists with respect to the legibility of printing types, the spacing of words within the lines and of the lines in relation to each other, the effect upon the eye of various stocks of print paper, and similar matters of immediate concern that obviate many classroom problems and, ofttimes even un- known to the teacher, materially lighten the burdens of daily instruction. Only experts know the great amount of detailed thought and enormous expense involved in producing the millions of Heath books that reach the hands of students and teachers year after year. The expressions of satisfaction, however, evoked by the fitting typography, pleasing appearance, and durable as well as artistic binding of these publications more than compen- sate for such labor, thought, and expense.

A veteran editor in his reminiscences has remarked: "It is interesting to recall the various relations we have had with an institution like D. C. Heath and Company since it was created, and with those who have continued to build it into a great temple for the promotion of learning."

"An institution—a temple of learning." It has been said that of the more than one hundred million persons in the United States above six years of age, one-half of those born in this country have used schoolbooks with the name of D. C. Heath and Company on the title-page.

Since 1885, when it began with only 24 titles, the House of Heath has published nearly 3000 books, and its list of subjects covers the entire educational field from the lowest primary grade through the university. "Tall oaks from little acorns grow."

During forty years of service D. C. Heath and Company has taken pride in its spirit of pioneering in the cause of education, in the standards of excellence motivating its publications, in its cordial relations with other publishers as well as in the good will and appreciation of all of its friends. The aim of the House of Heath is to continue to merit the confidence of the publishing world and of the many thousands of teachers throughout the country by maintaining its record of integrity and holding fast its place in the educational vanguard.